August 1996

For Susan

fine writer
in the spirit of
deep earth & soul

BEST,

[signature]

TIERRA ZIA

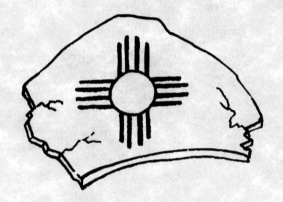

Gary David

Pen & Ink Drawings by Dawn Senior

NINE MUSES BOOKS

SEATTLE 1996

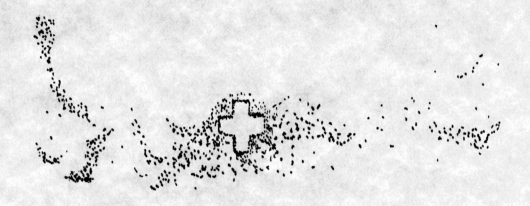

The author would like to thank
Haight Ashbury Literary Journal, Pemmican, South Ash Press, Synaesthetic,
W'ORCs and *The Spirit That Wants Me: A New Mexico Anthology*
for previously publishing a few of these poems.

The illustrations in this book were drawn by Dawn Senior
from photographs taken by the author.

Front cover: Tyuonyi ruins, Bandelier National Monument
Back cover: stone work façade on the Clear Light Opera House, Cerrillos, NM

nine muses books
3541 kent creek road
winston, or 97496

INTERLINEAL DEDICATION

This book began with our daughter
*   Zia Ann Descault David*
born a Leo (4:30 p. m. July 26, 1988)
*   Santa Fe, New Mexico.*

These lines seek to honor the Ancient Ones
*   whose work in stone quickens*
our love with a pure play
*   of light their turquoise skies intone.*

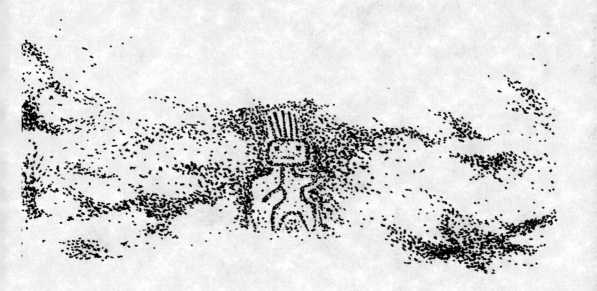

THE SPECTRAL SKIES IN NEW MEXICO

A blue so
quick it quivers
into indigo
everywhere
your eyes turn.
Into sere mouths
of mountains on the horizon
skies pour.
Into the hole
of a kiva (the sipapu)
beyond names
skies full
of blue
flames fall.
Blue puddles
on its floor
as smoking spirits
close the door.
Beyond sight
skies snake
underground streams down
your umbilical road
to the first world.
Mornings there are endless
blue mesas
of air.

TURNING SUMMER

After reading a long time about deep
ecology, I step out on the porch.
The belly of midnight swells
a sweet breath of growth.
Stars' stridulations echo
all the nameless constellations
of crickets hugging crystal globes
of dew. I think of concentric spheres
the medieval cosmos spun, smell onion
in the garden. Inside, my child stirs
inside her dreaming mother
or his. It's a mystery which-
ever way we turn. Whisper syllables
from sacred circles, and stars begin to burn
in the eyes of the unborn.

MORNING AT TSANKAWI *

Across stone slabs
snakes of lightning slither
                    into the hole of the world
        before our own.

                Whirlpools arc
        into rock
                    migration routes
            which draw one
                inward
                still.

        The unblinking eye
        etched with fire
for over five hundred journeys of the sun
    to the south & back, as sire to song
        the Turquoise Shaman raises
                forever
        his arms in praise of light —
                his thunder prayer
                    for life seeds
                        of He-rain.

* Located between the Sangre de Cristo and Jemez Mountains of northern New Mexico,
Tsankawi (tsank-ah-WEE, meaning "gap of the sharp round cactus") was the home of a group
of Rio Grande Anasazi from the early 14th to the late 16th centuries. Upon this mesa they built
a rectangular pueblo of about 350 rooms, 2-3 stories high, enclosing a large courtyard. On the
south-facing cliffside, smaller "talus pueblos" were constructed adjoining a number of caves,
some of which appear to be ceremonial in nature. All the petroglyphs shown in this poem (as
well as the ones on p.6 and p.16) are representations of those found on the caprocks or inside
the caves of Tsankawi..

Across the mesa of sharp round cactus & sage, ancient days
    are scattered
               potsherds, geometrically intricate
                              echoes of poetry
the clean-shaven winds snatch away— restless
            as snapshot tourists. On the wavering horizon
blue mountain ranges drift like dreams
      of shivering aspens, spruce needles & ice crystals
                     melting into morning.

At Tsankawi, worms of fire writhe
    in the dust. Terraced rooms of mortared tuff
           tumble the rubble
    of a world where once
  the kachinas came to drink.
           Within the round red arms
of ten kivas, the Ancient Ones felt the mothering Mystery
          as sound
   & as sure as one's own
        heart beat. Each stone
sang a litany of pure rivers.
        Their green world was forever
   laughing & clean
     as leaves of corn
       a storm of white water leaves
    shining.

What drought or sacred sign
     scorched in some dry arroyo
       had driven them here
  so long ago?
      In the West they'd left behind
  the Yellow Corn Maiden— her brittle husks scraping
     against the stubble
        of the wind's face.

Upon the village's path
        ages of aching arches
    on bare soles
or sandals made of yucca
      came to abrade
    a sandstone track— in places
up to two feet deep. Up to the mesa
    the Hump-Back Flute Player
      leads us, skipping
              satyr-like
      through rocks & cedar brakes
sowing his sack of seeds.
      Blowing a trickling melody
            of kisses
    into the honeyed heart
of a flowering cloud
        he dips
      his hummingbird beak
        to make
    the She-rains come.
With songs soft as a fawn's ear
      this pied piper of Tsankawi
        lured the children off somewhere
      so long ago
beyond the misty rim
      of their rainbow world.

At noon
a flock of raven-like heat waves
forces a dizzy retreat
to cool-tongued shadows
of cliffside caves.
In the haze to the South
Turtle Mountain* drifts
at the red edge
of the once-sacred world.
One's gaze grows dim
as a smoky flake
of obsidian.

Upon the soot-darkened wall
of a dank womb
of rock
the Plumed Serpent stirs
the tap root
in the blood.
Surrounding everyone
his return
begins to shimmer without beginning
or ending.

*Sandia Peak, near Albuquerque.

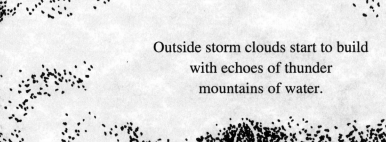

Outside storm clouds start to build
with echoes of thunder
mountains of water.

                    Older
                            than words

    the drumbeat of life
          dangles
                strips of fox fur
                        & feathers
          & dances
                            in hearts
                  open
    to the sun-sown footsteps
                of the coming raindrops.

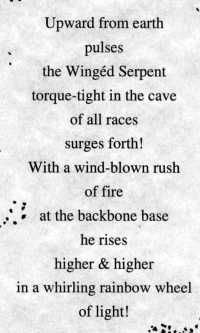

Upward from earth
pulses
the Wingéd Serpent
torque-tight in the cave
of all races
surges forth!
With a wind-blown rush
of fire
at the backbone base
he rises
higher & higher
in a whirling rainbow wheel
of light!

Across the hills of heaven
rolling
tumbling coils
of roiling sounds
the soaring serpent makes
his rounds
with lightning tongues
& cracks the clouds
like a giant rumbling
rawhide whip.

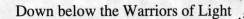

                    Down below the Warriors of Light
          lift
seed-bright & shining arms
              to receive
          the sacred sign
                    of the Rainbow Gift.

Above the blue Bear Mountain*
                    the Dipper pours
                              its milk of stars
          southward. The scales
              of the Plumed Snake
                              gleam
    in the dark
              & wandering eyes
                    of the war-weary children
              seeking
          the coming dream.

                    * San Antonio Mountain, near the Colorado/New Mexico border.

THE RIVER WITHIN THE TREE

birth poem for Zia Ann

Between the wave of each contraction
your mother had gone so far away
tiny clouds hung on the horizon
of her eyes.

Belly bulging like the burl
of a great elm, she rooted herself
and bore down. The weight
of the whole watery world
inside, her trunk split and
a river poured out.
Upon the shore of afternoon
you tumbled, gasping the blue
puddle of sky at your chin.

You've come from so far away.
From deep within
the oldest forest of wings
your heart would ever dream, you drifted
nine rippling moons
downstream— drawn here
by the conchshell call
of a song-drunk sun.

16

Love, the name of the river
is yours alone. The tree of the world
is ours together: the Great Mother.
Listen! Before she leaves
her perch, a yellow bird warbles
softer than the water
I weep on your cheek.
The branch springs back, quick
as new wings swirling
in the swelling flock
of her tears.

ST. FRANCIS FEEDS THE BAG LADY

She'll never swallow his vow
of poverty. She drinks
his spirit in a cold shadow
of the oldest house.
Now he wouldn't last
one night in his namesake:
La Villa Real de la Santa Fe
de San Francisco de Assisi.

The painted birds
forsake her shoulder.
Silver lining turquoise
eyes, bronze tourists flock
to patronize the arts.
Perched on a cloudy curb
of gallery alley, she whispers
to fluttering fingers
words torn like bread crumbs
from the foreign language
of her life. No sisters
in sight, she's lost in a forest
by others' more conspicuous
consumption. They spot
a goblet of leaded crystal
instead of darker faces.

A quainter painting shows
the blind faith of the famous
archbishop. He's feeding his masses
of pidgin Indians. They've come
to depend on him and vice
versa. Against the dark
wings which daily drop
upon our bag lady
of Guadalupe St., his mission
was a nippy Sunday picnic
in Cathedral Park.

Her mouth opens and the tongue
cracks the bell in the tower.
She knows each hour of hunger
thin as a wafer of light.
From a bloody century
the friar blesses her
final bottle of Thunderbird.

San Miguel Chapel, Santa Fe

CORONADO ON THE INTERSTATE (AT KUAUA RUINS)

If I sat
    near this jade slate
        of water sliding south—
If I sat here
    with ragged scraps of Rio
        crow songs in my ear—
If I sat here long
    beside the banked fires of cottonwoods'
        humming buds in a March wind—
If I sat here long enough
    across from Turtle Mountain dusted
        by morning snow and piñon—
If I sat here long enough I might
    against a thousand indigenas driven
        toward the Seven Cities of Cíbola—
If I sat here long enough I might find
    above a feathered heartbeat
        thumping drums in the mud—
If I sat here long enough I might find a poem.

If I sat here longer
    under bloody colors dancing
dream creatures within
    a smoking prayer hole*

*The "Painted Kiva" at Coronado National Monument near Bernalillo, New Mexico contains a series of fresco murals done by the Pueblo people long before the conquistador Francisco Vázquez de Coronado arrived to spend the winter of 1540-41.

I'd need to do no more
  than bless these bones
of a deer on the shore
  with corn pollen— let them
slip into the river
  fast as sleep.

But no, I am Coronado
on the interstate
to El Dorado— a shadow
skin of a rattlesnake
the fallen sun has shed.

OPPIE: *TAT TVAM ASI* (THOU ART THAT.)

Sporting porkpie hat and puffing
professorial pipe, prophet-like he gazes—
eyes glowing toward critical mass
across Pajarito Plateau. Sanskrit phrases
quantum leapfrog chalkdust equations
in dry arroyos. The *Gita* echoes
ponderosa pine and piñon
whispers. He knows the bloody skull
necklace Kali wears— just as well
as the devil's own chain reactions
plutonium (two thirty nine) unlocks. At dawn
on a blackboard mesa, this weary scarecrow
stalks among scattered potsherds
of Anasazi corn country, searching for a theory
which will hold heavy water.
                              Above Frijoles Cañon
at noon, the match-blue sky strikes
an eagle's eye. In the crumbling honeycomb
of the ruins, the Blue Star Kachina
starts his heart to pulse in time
to the round dance dynamo of the open kiva.

Now the western mountains breathe deep
in the night. Ancestors form a circle
into the Fifth World. Oppie bolts upright
in bed, each bead of sweat a crystal
humming high frequencies
on his forehead.

      He has seen the end
      of his dream: a gourd rattle
      of fire and thunder rises.
      For the first time ever
      he is shaken.

BLEEDING BLUE FIRE

Last night I lay in a concrete cage
no larger than those cardboard shacks
the homeless build beneath the thunder
of urban bridges. Cobwebs and cracks
snaked with urine, its bed chilled
my haunches like a morgue's slab.
Naked and dusty, a low-watt lightbulb
my only heat. No window. Smells
of musty breath and bread mold
crept across my pillow. Rats
with gray armadillo scales kept
running on my chest. All night
I lay in a concrete cage.

Today I'm trapped in the distance
the Sangre de Cristo brings to my eyes.
In waves, sapphire on indigo, they lift.
There must be justice somewhere
I whisper— somewhere within
their arms of spruce and fir.
Beyond cloudy mountains bleeding
blue fire through canyons of sky
there must be a clearing—
some quiet place
                    the sun is born.

TRINITY CITATIONS

I: J. Robert Oppenheimer

The Fruit in the Midst of the Garden
(Or, Why I Built the Gadget)

It was technically
sweet.

II: General Thomas F. Farrell

The Truth of the Matter

It was that beauty
the great poets dream about
but describe most poorly
and inadequately.

III: Edward Teller

Sinners in the Hands of An Angry Bomb

The things we are working on
are so terrible
no amount of protesting
or fiddling with politics
will save our souls.

THROUGH THE MOUTH OF CHACO CANYON*

-1-

Forlorn as an echo
of a shotgun, roofless rooms
at Pueblo Bonito, blasted
by sunlight and wind, recede
from our understanding.
We know the bolt action
of our own time, but don't succeed
in making whole again
these broken pots. On the curve of
a great kiva, dawn ignites
the longest day in a niche
of summer. A hidden passageway
to the center whispers
riddles in the dust to which
our radials have taken us.

Twenty miles over a washboard road
still leaves a nuclear family
in the middle of nowhere fast. I race
my wife and little girl to the scarp, stop
at masonry stairs climbing
toward places we'll never go. Dead clans left

*The site of Anasazi ruins in northwestern New Mexico. Pueblo Bonito and Chetro Ketl are
two major villages in this complex of multi-story, stone pueblos. Fajada Butte and Chacra
Mesa lie a few miles southeast of these structures. Until very recently a spiral petroglyph on
Fajada Butte precisely indicated solstice and equinox dates.

27

no maps to the crowded plaza
where we belong. We find instead
the sun dagger at Fajada Butte
no longer quarters the yellow squash
of the solar circle, shifted
by waffle-soled boots.

Layer upon chinked layer sealed
with caliche, stonework withstood
droughts and mounting centuries
of snowdrifts. A crow sweeps
his melting shadow over
ocher cliffs the same
morning a Norman duke crosses
the channel to Hastings.

-2-

As Nita and Zia giggle in the rubble
of Chetro Ketl, grinding pretend corn
on mano and metate, I lean against a wall—
its shadow shifting long after we've fallen
silent— and read about "The dearth
of human remains…" Not enough bones here
to flesh out the five hundred rooms. Behind us
stones chew the meal of years too slowly
for us to taste whatever sustained
across sagebrush miles on Chacra Mesa
the holy dances back to the heart.

Clouds crumble in golden light
the fallen pueblo sun gives.
Copper bells, turquoise beads, and macaw feathers
point elsewhere. We're farther away. Evening brings
news of another day to a motel in Grants.
Snacking on sugared cereal, our daughter aims
the remote to switch the channel.
A coyote drops another anvil
off a cliff. It keeps falling and falling
through dreams hours later, smashes
the skull of the last ancestor to bits
of black-on-white pottery.
Red star petroglyphs evaporate
from a rock face as I wake
to the white noise of an air conditioner.
To the east a gray blur
paves the road home— the only place
in all our ruins we've failed to find.

As I drive back, a commuter sun
wheels through a new adobe
supermarket in Albuquerque, blinding us
to kivas sleeping in the dark
of each sprouted bean.

The great kiva at Casa Rinconada

CLIMBING PUYÉ* CLIFFS

Talus scatters your footsteps
at the base of the mesa.
A light-headed climb toward the plaza
choked with ragweed and rabbitbrush
steals your breath.
Your spirit has forgotten
like a fallen brick
its dark house. Turned to dust
your heart no longer mourns
the hearth's ashes. A hush
over four centuries sifts
through thin, arthritic fingers
in the wind. Still
the painted shards recall
hands that shaped the jars
from red ancestral clay
of your homeland.

On broken vertebrae
of the village wall, a lizard waits
motionless— its head dull
as a crowbar. Pocked with black
viga holes, cliffs vanish
far beyond blank horizons
in its eyes. Quick as a gasp
it skitters into dead grass.

* The Puyé Cliff Dwellings are located near the Santa Clara Pueblo northwest of Santa Fe.

Through the dry clack
a hopper's wings make, you hear
the arrogant drone
from a distant airplane bore.
It sputters into dead clouds. You fear
it's headed for a high blue hangar
in the future.

TIERRA ZIA

"Ah Sun-flower! weary of time,
Who countest the steps of the Sun ..."

William Blake

Descending celestial the spiral staircase
between the spinal mountain ranges
(the twin kachinas) of New Mexico
down to the blood-channeled chapel
of Tierra Zia, alight on every leaf
and golden petal, opening
the heart as easily
as an obsidian knife, each note
in the unfolding melody
of life is an echo made
flesh: divine energy of the Son
of the Great Mystery incarnate
in the biomasses. Democratic vistas extending
to all species (grasses and primates alike)
countless choirs of sensual angels

sing as one!

Descending solar the crystal staircase
of time, stately as the lovely canon
Pachelbel spun, into the New World quincunx
of space, the Kin of Movement
comes: Awanyu*...

* Known as Kukulkan to the Mayas and Quetzalcoatl to the Aztecs, Awanyu was the name the
Tewa of northern New Mexico called the Feathered Snake. This representation is patterned after
a petroglyph at Tshirege ruins, located within the boundaries of Los Alamos National Laboratory.

... the Plumed Serpent
returns— his blinding vision of fission force
transformed. Over are the hell cycles and flywheels
of well-oiled machinations grinding to the fossil-fueled end
this millenium. Over the Sangre de Cristo
corona down and pollen dust mingle. The People
of all nations gather now in the sacred hoop
                             of the Rainbow Snake.
Ascending pineal the milk-smooth forehead
of the White Corn Maiden, Morning Star chants
new beginnings. Like the time-lapse
of the last sunflower, each hour blooms
an instant— each age a blink
of the dark eye raging
in the Sun of Man's heart. Rising
as the halo of the Holy Virgin, the red arms
of Zia
         reach out to bless the dawn
                        of sacred earth.

SKY CITY*

– 1 –

Scanning the telescoped landscape
for a language of feathered clouds
dreaming rock, we took an old bus
to the blue-roofed mesa top
of the zodiac. An Ácoma driver told us
how long, how cold nights arc
a river of stars where some of his clan
still winter. Under thin March sunlight
we walked their plaza: displaced voices
muted by late afternoon
sepia and dried blood. While kinship echoes
a thousand years on this parchment vista
dripping shadows, felt-tipped
verses would evaporate the moment
a melting moon cleared
the edge of her red world.

– 2 –

Cutting through the daily rote
with a sharp shard in her throat,
our tour guide's dark wind hissed
the hardest story of this
"oldest continuously inhabited city

*Ácoma Pueblo, about 70 miles west of Albuquerque.

in the U. S." Pointing skyward
she told how their poor children
got sold into slavery— all
so that brass mission bell
of San Estevan up there might toll
forever! (How many? It was many
years ago.) Might've been four
or seven —times ten?— little "people
of the white rock" taken away
to Tenochtitlán. Might've been
the Pleiades to which they flew for all
we or they knew or know.

– 3 –

Beyond the nova-headed nails
of a kiva ladder, alone above
the catch basin of green water stood
their star-hearted cottonwood— leafless as bone
dreaming rain. While our three-year-old
daughter Zia drifted off
softer than seed fluff
on her mother's shoulder, two little
Indian girls in mermaid T-shirts
by a beehive oven dug
through golden dust seeking
the yeast of years to come.

But we'd taste no warm bread
on the breeze nor turn red wine
into water on their tongues, hear
no deer songs that urge
blue or yellow corn up
from rainbow earth either.
No new clay pot or plate to adorn
our days, years ago
we just bought an ancient
brown and black on white
star-broken piece found at the base
of Enchanted Mesa to the east.

– 4 –

At dusk we took the hard way
down, the slow way— sleeping little
rosebud girl on our switched backs
on their toeholds hacked
from sunburst sandstone how many
years ago! How many spirit hands
eased us down, took our steps
down those cliffs! How many wings fluttered
hummingbird hearts until
the tingle of soles stopped
at the unpurchased foot of that
precarious stairway. We make

     the hard way, the slow way
     still: spiral
     arms of the farthest Sky City
     calling us home.

THE DIFFERENCES

From white apricot blossoms my eyes
lift —the luminous blue distances—
to sun-bright snowdrifts in the heart

of the Sangre de Cristo. Groping
down a dirt road, shadows crawl
adobe walls. Ristras drip red

on turquoise doorways. From the blood
a thousand conquistadores sung
to the Anglo's bones flowering

at Ghost Ranch —like the thread
of a spinning spider— a dust devil hung
between thorny whispers thirsts

to dance over the differences.

ENVOI: TOUCHING THE TEACHER

My daughter dancing, her eyes
learn the ways of the world
as she follows the line on the first map
she makes with a purple pen:

Slumberland, Castle of Evil Wizards,
Island of Faeries, Island of the Princess
she says she is. Dreamland...
"That's much bigger than the world,"

I say. Through cloud gauze
on the evening horizon, the sun clots.
"Why do we live in this planet?"
She whirls the indigo veil

of her wings, skips and leaps a tipsy
pirouette. "To learn to do
things, to learn..." but
tired of talk, she breezes off

before I can add: "to love—
to love before we leave."